BASEBALL STARS

Coloring book

NATIONAL LEAGUE

YADIER MOLINA

7

CHRISTIAN YELICH

9

KYLE HENDRICKS

11

JOEY VOTTO

BRYCE HARPER

23

MOOKIE BETTS

27

BRANDON BELT

31

KRIS BRYANT

33

AMERICAN LEAGUE

RANDY AROZARENA

41

45

BALTIMORE ORIOLES

JOSE RAMIREZ

51

DYLAND CEASE

SALVADOR PEREZ

55

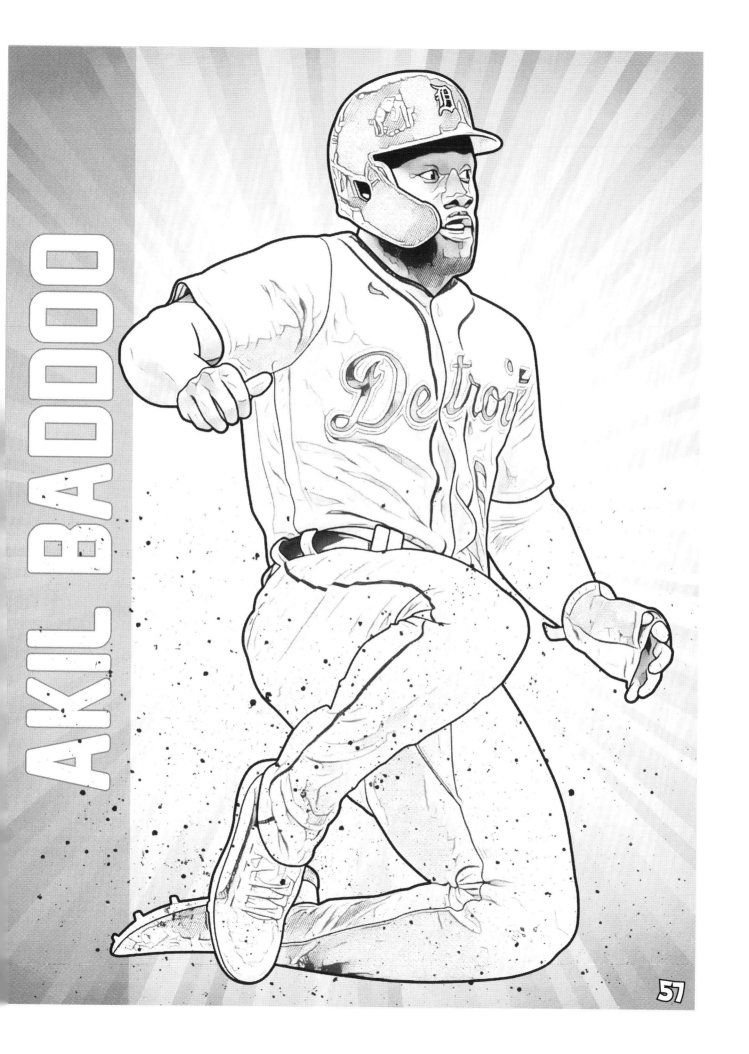

ALEX BREGMAN

59

COREY SEAGER

63

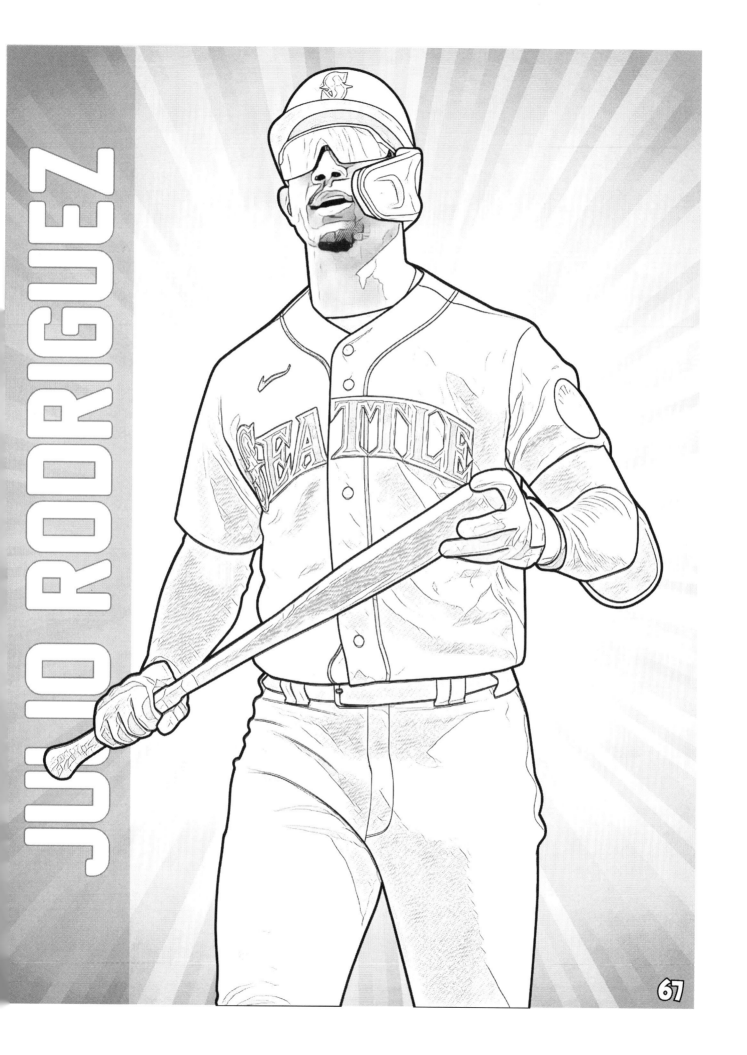

JULIO RODRIGUEZ

67

INDEX

DRAKE LONDON

ATLANTA
FALCONS

75

LAMAR JACKSON

BALTIMORE
RAVENS

77

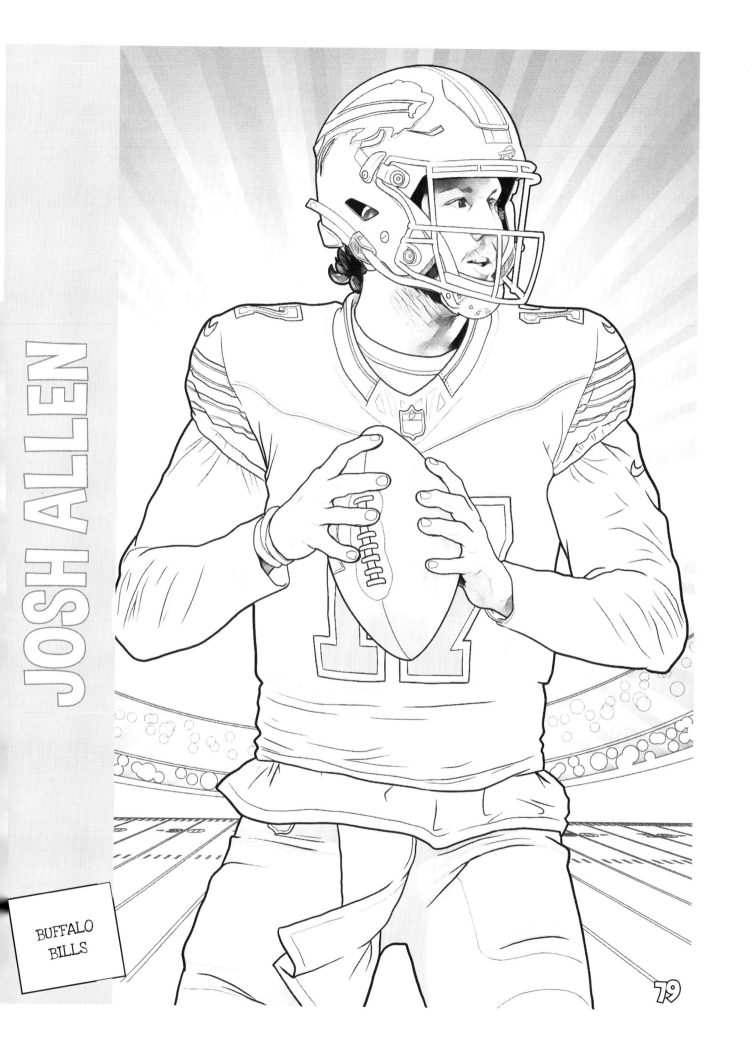

JOSH ALLEN

BUFFALO
BILLS

79

BRYCE YOUNG

CAROLINA
PANTHERS

JUSTIN FIELDS

CHICAGO
BEARS

83

JOE BURROW

CINCINNATI BENGALS

85

MICAH PARSONS

DALLAS
COWBOYS

PATRICK SURTAIN

DENVER
BRONCOS

91

JORDAN LOVE

GREEN BAY PACKERS

PATRICK MAHOMES

KANSAS CITY

DAVANTE ADAMS

LAS VEGAS RAIDERS

105

JUSTIN HERBERT

LOS ANGELES
CHARGERS

107

MATTHEW STAFRFORD

LOS ANGELES
RAMS

109

RHAMONDRE STEVENSON

NEW ENGLAND PATRIOTS

115

DEREK CARR

NEW ORLEANS
SAINTS

SAQUON BARKLEY

NEW YORK
GIANTS

T.J. WATT

PITTSBURGH STEELERS

125

NICK BOSA

SAN
FRANCISCO
49ERS

DK METCALF

SEATTLE
SEAHAWKS

129

TRISTAN WIRFS

TAMPA BAY
BUCCANEERS

TERRY MCLAURIN

WASHINGTON
FOOTBALL

INDEX

EASTERN CONFERENCE

143

153

155

WESTERN CONFERENCE

I hope you enjoyed the book.
If you liked it, please leave us a good review
on Amazon and your comments so that we
can keep improving.

We really appreciate your feedback
and will be happy to implement your
recommendations.

Made in the USA
Monee, IL
02 November 2024

69173132R00114